BILL BRYSON'S
AFRICAN DIARY

www.**billbryson**.co.uk

By Bill Bryson

THE LOST CONTINENT

MOTHER TONGUE

TROUBLESOME WORDS

NEITHER HERE NOR THERE

MADE IN AMERICA

NOTES FROM A SMALL ISLAND
(published in the USA as *I'm a Stranger Here Myself*)

A WALK IN THE WOODS

NOTES FROM A BIG COUNTRY

DOWN UNDER
(published in the USA as *In a Sunburned Country*)

AFRICAN DIARY

A SHORT HISTORY OF NEARLY EVERYTHING

THE LIFE AND TIMES OF THE THUNDERBOLT KID

SHAKESPEARE
(Eminent Lives series)

BRYSON'S DICTIONARY FOR WRITERS AND EDITORS

ICONS OF ENGLAND

AT HOME

ONE SUMMER

THE ROAD TO LITTLE DRIBBLING

BILL BRYSON'S

AFRICAN DIARY

A SHORT TRIP FOR A WORTHY CAUSE

Doubleday

LONDON · TORONTO · SYDNEY · AUCKLAND · JOHANNESBURG

TRANSWORLD PUBLISHERS
61–63 Uxbridge Road, London W5 5SA
www.transworldbooks.co.uk

Transworld is part of the Penguin Random House group of companies
whose addresses can be found at global.penguinrandomhouse.com

Penguin
Random House
UK

First published in Great Britain in 2002 by Doubleday
an imprint of Transworld Publishers
Doubleday edition reissued 2016

A CIP catalogue record for this book
is available from the British Library.

ISBN
9780857524201

Printed and bound by Clays Ltd, Bungay, Suffolk.

Penguin Random House is committed to a sustainable
future for our business, our readers and our planet. This book
is made from Forest Stewardship Council® certified paper.

3 5 7 9 10 8 6 4 2

BILL BRYSON'S
AFRICAN DIARY

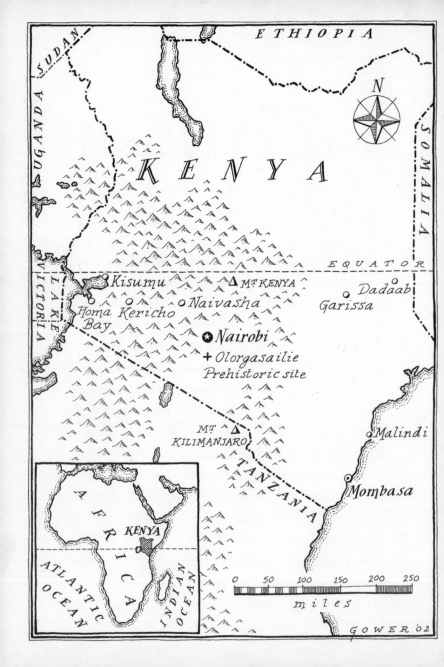

In the late 1940s and early 1950s, after he became a little too saggy to fit into a Tarzan loincloth without depressing popcorn sales among cinema audiences, the great Johnny Weissmuller filled the twilight years of his acting career with a series of low-budget adventure movies with titles like *Devil Goddess* and *Jungle Moon Men*, all built around a character called Jungle Jim. These modest epics are largely forgotten now, which is a pity because they were possibly the most cherishably terrible movies ever made. The plots seldom got anywhere near coherence. My own favourite, called *Pygmy Island*, involved a lost tribe of white midgets and a strange but valiant fight against the spread of Communism. But the narrative possibilities were practically infinite since each Jungle Jim feature consisted in large measure of scenes taken from other, wholly unrelated adventure movies. Whatever footage was available – train

crashes, volcanic eruptions, rhino charges, panic scenes
involving large crowds of Japanese – would be snipped
from the original and woven into Jungle Jim's wondrously
accommodating story lines. From time to time, the ever-
more-fleshy Weissmuller would appear on the scene to
wrestle the life out of a curiously rigid and unresisting
crocodile or chase some cannibals into the woods, but
these intrusions were generally brief and seldom entirely
explained.

I wouldn't be at all surprised to learn that no more than
four people at a time ever paid money to watch a Jungle
Jim movie. The series might well have escaped my own
attention except that in about 1959 WOI-TV, a television
station well known in central Iowa for its tireless commit-
ment to mediocrity, acquired the complete Jungle Jim
oeuvre and for the next dozen or so years showed two
of them back to back late every Friday night. What is
especially tragic about all this is that I not only watched
these movies with unaccountable devotion, but was
indelibly influenced by them. In fact, were it not for some
scattered viewings of the 1952 classic *Bwana Devil* and a
trip on the Jungle Safari ride at Disneyland in 1961, my
knowledge of African life, I regret to say, would be entirely
dependent on Jungle Jim movies.

I can't say it actively preyed on me that my impressions of Africa were based so heavily on a series of B-movies made in California more than half a century ago, but when a personable young man named Dan McLean from the London office of CARE International, the venerable and worthy charity, asked me if I would be willing to go to Kenya to visit some of their projects and write a few words on their behalf, it occurred to me that there were some gaps in my familiarity with the Dark Continent that I might usefully fill in. So I agreed.

Some weeks later, I was summoned to CARE's London offices for a meeting with Dan, his boss Will Day and a rugged and amiable fellow named Nick Southern, CARE's regional manager in east Africa, who happened to be in London at the time. We sat around a big table spread with maps of Kenya, while they outlined what they had in mind for me.

'Of course, you'll have to fly to the refugee camp at Dadaab,' Will observed thoughtfully at one point. He glanced at me. 'To avoid the bandits,' he explained.

Dan and Nick nodded gravely.

'I beg your pardon?' I said, taking a sudden interest.

'It's bandit country all round there,' Will said.

'Where?' I asked, peering at the map for the first time.

'Oh, just there,' Will said, waving a hand vaguely across most of east Africa. 'But you'll be fine in a plane.'

'They only rarely shoot at planes,' Nick explained.

This wasn't at all what I had had in mind, frankly. By way of homework, I had dutifully watched *Out of Africa*, from which I derived the impression that this trip would mostly take place on a veranda somewhere while turbaned servants brought me lots of coffee. I knew that we would probably visit a clinic from time to time and that someone in the party might occasionally have to shoot a charging animal, but I hadn't imagined anything shooting at me in return.

'So how dangerous is Kenya then?' I asked in a small, controlled squeak.

'Oh, not at all,' they responded in unison.

'Well, hardly,' Will added.

'It depends on what you mean by dangerous, of course,' said Dan.

'Like bleeding and not getting up again,' I suggested. 'Being shot and stabbed and so forth,' I added.

They assured me that that only very rarely happened, and that it was nearly always one or the other. You had to be very unlucky to be shot and stabbed, they said.

'It's mostly diseases you have to worry about,' Nick went

on. 'Malaria, schistosomiasis, trypanosomiasis…'

'Rift Valley fever, blackwater fever, yellow fever…' said Dan.

'Dengue fever, bilharzia – the usual tropical stuff,' added Will.

But they pointed out that you can be inoculated against many of those and for the rest most people manage a more or less complete recovery, given time and a considered programme of physiotherapy. Many even walk again. I asked if there was anything else I should know.

'Well, the roads are a little dangerous – there are some crazy drivers out there,' Will said, chuckling.

'But apart from that and the diseases and the bandits and the railway from Nairobi to Mombasa, there's absolutely nothing to worry about,' Nick added.

'What's wrong with the railway?'

'Oh, nothing really. It's just the rolling stock is a little antiquated and sometimes the brakes give out coming down out of the mountains – but, hey, if you worried about all the things that might happen you wouldn't go anywhere, would you?'

'I don't go anywhere,' I pointed out.

They nodded thoughtfully.

'Well, it'll be an adventure,' Will said brightly. 'You'll

be fine, absolutely fine. Just check your insurance before you go.'

And so it was that I became irrevocably committed to the African adventure which follows.

SATURDAY, 28 SEPTEMBER 2002

We meet at the Kenya Airways check-in desk at Heathrow, the five brave souls who are to form our party from London. In addition to me and Dan, they are: David Sanderson, a thoughtful and kindly fellow who is soon to take up a post in Johannesburg as CARE's regional manager in southern and western Africa, but joins us now in his capacity as urban specialist; Justin Linnane, an intent but amiable young maker of television documentaries who has volunteered to make a video record of the expedition; and the photographer Jenny Matthews, whose brilliant and compassionate snaps grace this volume. White-haired and sweetly unobtrusive, Jenny is easily the wonder of the lot. If you saw her in a supermarket you would take her for a schoolteacher or civil servant. In fact, for twenty-five years she has gone wherever there is danger – to Chechnya, Bosnia, Afghanistan, Rwanda. She is fearless and evidently indestructible. If things go bad on this trip, it is her I'll hold on to.

The first good news is that Kenya Airways has given us all an upgrade on account of our genial goodness and dapper manner, and so of course gets a glowing mention here. It is a nine-and-a-half-hour flight from London to Nairobi, and we are very pleased to pass it in comfort, with a better class of drinks and our own party packs.

An hour or so after we are airborne by chance I come across an article in *The Economist* declaring Nairobi to be the new crime capital of Africa. My attention is particularly arrested by the disclosure that street children come up to cars waiting at traffic lights demanding money and if it's not given they rub balls of human excrement in their victims' faces.

I share this information with my new companions and we agree that Dan, as group leader, will be our designated 'rubbee' for the week. Conveniently, Dan is in the lavatory when the matter is discussed and so the motion carries unanimously. In order not to spoil his enjoyment of Nairobi we decide not to tell him of our decision until we see children advancing.

It is nighttime when we land at Jomo Kenyatta Airport and

pleasantly cool. We are met by Kentice Tikolo, an immensely good-natured Kenyan lady who helps run CARE's Nairobi
office and who shepherds us into waiting cabs. In *Out of
Africa*, Nairobi was depicted as a sunny little country town,
so I am disappointed to find that at some time in the past
fifty or sixty years they took away that pretty scene and
replaced it with Omaha, of all things. Nairobi is merely yet
another modern city with traffic lights and big buildings
and hoardings advertising Samsung televisions and the like.
Our hotel is a Holiday Inn – very nice and comfortable, but
hardly a place that shouts: 'Welcome to Africa, Bwana.'

'Oh, you will see plenty of Africa,' Kentice assures me
when we convene at the bar for a round of medicinal
hydration. 'We're going to show you lots of exotic things.
Have you ever eaten camel?'

'Only in my junior high school cafeteria, and they called
it lamb,' I reply. I take the opportunity, while Dan is at the
bar, to ask her about the street children I read about on the
flight.

'Oh, that's the least of your worries,' Kentice laughs. 'Car-
jackings are much worse. They can be quite violent.'

'What a comfort to know.'

'But don't worry,' she says, laying a comforting hand on
my arm and becoming solemn, 'if anything goes wrong we

have excellent hospitals in Nairobi.'

We retire early because we have an early start in the morning. I am disappointed to find that there is no mosquito net around the bed in my room. Unaware that Nairobi is malaria-free, I slather myself with insect repellent and pass a long night sounding like two strips of parting Velcro each time I roll over in the bed and dreaming terrible dreams in which Jungle Jim, assisted by a tribe of white pygmies, chases me through the streets of Omaha with dung balls.

SUNDAY, 29 SEPTEMBER

In the morning we drive to Kibera, a sea of tin roofs filling a mile or so of steamy hillside on the south side of the city. Kibera is the biggest slum in Nairobi, possibly the biggest in Africa. Nobody knows how many people live there. It's at least 700,000, but it may be as many as a million, perhaps more. At least fifty thousand of Kibera's children are AIDS orphans. At least a fifth of the residents are HIV positive, but it could be as high as fifty per cent. Nobody knows. Nothing about Kibera is certain and official, including its existence. It appears on no maps. It just is.

You can't just go into Kibera if you are an outsider. Well, you can, but you wouldn't come out again. Kibera is a dangerous place. We were taken on a walking tour by the district chief, an amiable giant named Nashon Opiyo, and three of his deputies, all Kibera residents. They are employed by the government to keep an eye – and occasionally a lid – on things, even though Kibera doesn't officially exist.

'To step into Kibera is to be lost at once in a random, seemingly endless warren of rank, narrow passageways wandering between rows of frail, dirt-floored hovels made of tin and mud and twigs and holes. Each shanty, on average, is ten feet by ten and home to five or six people. Down the centre of each lane runs a shallow trench filled with a trickle of water and things you don't want to see or step in. There are no services in Kibera – no running water, no rubbish collection, virtually no electricity, not a single flush toilet. In one section of Kibera called Laini Saba until recently there were just ten pit latrines for 40,000 people. Especially at night when it is unsafe to venture out, many residents rely on what are known as 'flying toilets', which is to say they go into a plastic bag, then open their door and throw it as far as possible.

In the rainy season, the whole becomes a liquid ooze. In

the dry season it has the charm and healthfulness of a rubbish tip. In all seasons it smells of rot. It's a little like wandering through a privy. Whatever is the most awful place you have ever experienced, Kibera is worse.

Kibera is only one of about a hundred slums in Nairobi, and it is by no means the worst. Altogether more than half of Nairobi's three million people are packed into these immensely squalid zones, which together occupy only about 1.5 per cent of the city's land. In wonder I asked David Sanderson what made Kibera superior.

'There are a lot of factories around here,' he said, 'so there's work, though nearly all of it is casual. If you're lucky you might make a few dollars a day, enough to buy a little food and a jerry can of water and to put something aside for your rent.'

'How much is rent?'

'Oh, not much. Ten or twelve dollars a month. But the average annual income in Kenya is $280, so $120 or $140 in rent every year is a big slice of your income. And nearly everything else is expensive here, too, even water. The average person in a slum like Kibera pays five times what people in the developed world pay for the same volume of water piped to their homes.'

'That's amazing,' I said.

He nodded. 'Every time you flush a toilet you use more water than the average person in the developing world has for all purposes in a day – cooking, cleaning, drinking, everything. It's very tough. For a lot of people Kibera is essentially a life sentence. Unless you are exceptionally lucky with employment, it's very, very difficult to get ahead.'

Every day around the world, 180,000 people fetch up in or are born into cities like Nairobi, mostly into slums like Kibera. Ninety per cent of the world's population growth in the twenty-first century will be in cities.

'For better or worse, this is where the future is,' David said. Yet, amazingly, aid agencies like CARE can do little for urban slums like Kibera. The governments won't let them. 'Mostly they won't permit any kind of permanent improvements because they fear it would just affirm Kibera's existence, and also they are afraid that it would encourage more people to pour in from the countryside. So they'd rather pretend these places don't exist.'

'But they must know it's here.'

He smiled and pointed to a big house – a compound – commanding a neighbouring hillside only a couple of hundred yards from Kibera's edge. The house, David told me, was the Nairobi residence of Daniel arap Moi, president of Kenya since 1978. 'This is what he sees every morning when he looks out his window. Of course they know it's here.'

Walking along with us was one of our minders, a kindly man of indeterminate age named Bonard Onyango. I asked him if he had always lived in Kibera.

'Oh no,' he said. 'I came here from the country twenty years ago.'

'How bad can the country be that you'd prefer this?' I asked.

'The country is very nice,' he agreed, 'but there's no work there and so no money. If you have no money, you can't send your children to school. But in the city if you work hard and you are lucky you can educate your children and maybe they will have a better life. All these people, they are here for their children.'

'Really?' I said.

'Oh, yes. Most of them.'

Kentice had been listening to this and was nodding in agreement. 'Just over there,' she said, pointing vaguely along some rooftops, 'is the Olympic Primary School. Do you know, it is the best primary school in all of Kenya?'

'Truly?' I said, impressed.

She nodded gravely. 'Three of the eight top-scoring primary schools in the country are here in Kibera. People from outside Kibera try to get their children into these schools because they are so good.' She nodded some more. 'People here will do anything to improve the lot of their children.'

'So it's not completely hopeless?' I said.

Kentice gave a big laugh. 'Oh, no,' she said. 'In Kenya we always have hope.'

In the afternoon, just to make sure the contrast was total, we drove out to the western edge of the city through a succession of wooded suburbs that seemed to owe more to Guildford or Weybridge than to Africa. Our destination was a formerly all-white preserve called Karen, whose most famous resident was also, though coincidentally, called Karen. I refer to Karen Blixen of *Out of Africa* fame.

We stopped at the Karen Blixen Coffee Garden, built around an old farmhouse that was once part of her coffee plantation, and is now a popular spot for Sunday lunch. After Kibera anything would seem good, but this was almost painfully agreeable. Inside the farmhouse a lavishly varied buffet was spread out and outside, scattered around a large shady lawn, were tables of all sizes, mostly occupied by feasting white families. It can't have been greatly different in colonial times.

After lunch we strolled the few hundred yards up the road to Blixen's house, the setting for much of *Out of Africa*. I can't say I was hugely interested in the personal history of Karen Blixen, but it was an interesting insight into the privileged lifestyles of the colonial period – which, not incidentally, didn't last all that long: only about sixty years. Blixen herself spent only seventeen years in Kenya, barely a fifth of her life. Anyway, it was a very pleasant house and the grounds were gorgeous, with long views across to Blixen's blue and beloved Ngong Hills. My big excitement, however, was that as we were walking back to the car I saw my first Maasai – a young man with a long walking stick and a bolt of red cloth wrapped around his waist and draped over a shoulder – loping past on the other side of the road. It seemed almost preposterously unreal to see a genuine African icon walking through this little lost corner of Surrey.

'What's he doing here?' I asked, surprised.

Kentice looked at me with a touch of wonder. 'He lives here,' she said. 'It's his country.'

MONDAY, 30 SEPTEMBER

Knowing of my interest in ancient pre-humans (because of a book I have been working on), Kentice set up a visit to the National Museum. There we met Dr Emma Mbua, the petite and cheerful chief palaeoanthropologist. Thanks largely to the efforts of two generations of the Leakey family, the museum has the finest collection of early human remains in existence.

It is an exceedingly rare event when a human bone fossilizes – only about one in a billion does so – and even rarer when one is found. You could easily fit all the early human bones that have ever been discovered into the back of a small delivery van. If you include every last tooth and chip of ancient bone ever found, only about 5,000 individuals have contributed to the human fossil record. Five hundred of these are held in the Kenyan National Museum in what is aptly known as the Strong Room, a slightly oversized version of a bank vault, with a heavy steel door and thick windowless walls. It is the greatest single hoard in the world, more priceless by far than any collection of royal baubles. Almost never is a non-specialist allowed into this room. I was honoured indeed.

All the specimens are kept in small wooden chests in

cupboards lined up around the walls. For one giddy hour, Dr Mbua brought out one celebrated skull after another. Here was the first *Homo habilis*, found by Louis Leakey in 1964 and long thought to be our earliest direct ancestor. Then came the famous *Australopithecus boisei*, 1.6 million years old and found miraculously intact, lying on the ground in the open, by Louis's son Richard in 1969. Then there was the extraordinary Turkana boy, whose nearly complete skeleton was found in northern Kenya in the 1980s and which at a stroke provided scientists with more *Homo erectus* bones than all the previous finds put together.

Dr Mbua's most treasured relic was a nineteen-million-year-old skull of an ape known as *proconsul*. 'It was sent to the British Museum for cleaning in the 1940s,' she said, 'and it took us forty years to persuade them to return it.'

'Why?' I asked.

'They coveted it,' she said, smiling serenely, but hinting at levels of darkness in the world of palaeontology that I hadn't known existed. 'Now we don't let anything leave the museum, ever. They are too delicate and too precious. If you want to see any of these special things, you must come to Nairobi.' How glad I was that I had.

* * *

The scarcity of human remains isn't just because few bones become fossils, but also because precious few landscapes offer the right conditions to preserve fossils. The greatest of them is the Great Rift Valley, and it was there we headed next.

I had always imagined the Rift Valley as some kind of canyon – a comparatively confined space where your voice would echo off walls of rock. In fact, it is a mighty plain, a hundred miles or so across and four thousand miles long. It is immense, and startlingly sumptuous in its beauty. As you head south and west out of Nairobi there comes a place where the ground just falls away and there spread out below you is the biggest open space you have ever seen: the Great Rift Valley. It is an amazing sight – a pale green vastness interrupted here and there by dead volcanic craters, but otherwise infinite and flat and very hot looking.

We were headed for a place called Olorgasailie, sixty miles beyond the Ngong Hills on the valley floor. When we arrived, we stepped from the vehicle into a dry, oven-like heat, which was all the more startling after the comparative coolness of Nairobi. In 1919, a geologist named J. W. Gregory was poking around in the area when he came across an expanse of ancient and distinctive teardrop-shaped hand axes of a type known as Acheulean. In the

1940s, Louis Leakey and his wife, Mary, got around to excavating the site. What they found was that Olorgasailie was a kind of factory where these tools were made in incalculable numbers over about a million years, from 1.2 million to 200,000 years ago. But here's the thing. The stones from which the axes were made aren't found on the Rift Valley floor. They had to be brought there from two nearby mountains named Ol Esakut and Mount Olorgasailie, each about ten kilometres away. Why the early people went to such trouble and what exactly they used the tools for have long been a mystery. Acheulean axes were beautiful pieces of technology for the time, and each represented a lot of effort to create, but they weren't outstandingly good for cutting or chopping or scraping – certainly not a great deal better than almost any random unshaped rock would be.

Yet for a million years early humans went to the considerable trouble of collecting and carrying large hunks of quartz and obsidian miles across a baking landscape to make them into axes at this one ten-acre site. More than this, the excavations showed that there was one area where axes were made and another where worn axes were brought to be re-sharpened. It was all amazingly organized.

Today, thousands upon thousands of these stone tools

are heaped and scattered everywhere around Olorgasailie, left where they were dropped hundreds of thousands of years ago by ancestors so remote from us that they weren't yet even *Homo sapiens*. It is an extraordinary site. One other curiosity is that no human remains have ever been found at Olorgasailie. We have to guess who the early people were.

I know all this because a very bright and enthusiastic young man named Jillani Ngalla from the Kenyan National Museum conducted us around the site. Ngalla appeared to know everything there is to know about Olorgasailie, Acheulean tools, the Rift Valley, and early hominids, and yet he seemed awfully young for an authority. I asked him how long he had been a palaeontologist.

'Oh, I'm not,' he said cheerfully. 'I am an aspiring palaeontologist. I've been accepted at the University of Pretoria,' he added with a touch of pride, 'but sadly I don't have the necessary funds.'

'How much would it cost?' I asked.

'Ten thousand US dollars.' He gave me an apologetic look, as if he had just said ten million.

'And do you have any hope of getting that kind of money?' I asked.

'As things stand at the moment,' he answered and

considered the question carefully for a minute, 'no.'

In the early evening we made our way to the modestly grand central railway station in Nairobi to catch the overnight sleeper to Mombasa. Kenya Railways has something of a tradition of killing its passengers. In just the past decade, a little over two hundred people have died in accidents on its trains. The accident that seems to have attracted the most publicity in recent years was one in 1999 when the overnight Nairobi-to-Mombasa train jumped the rails at an interesting-sounding place called 'Man Eaters' Junction', in Tsavo National Park, killing thirty-two people.

The crew blamed brake failure. Kenya Railways blamed the crew. No one really knows what happened. The following year another thirty-plus people were killed in two accidents, both involving runaway trains, in the space of four days. The biggest disaster of all was in 1993 when a train bound for Mombasa from Nairobi plunged off a bridge and into the 'crocodile-infested' Ngai Ndeithya River, killing 140 people. Ngai Ndeithya means 'God help us' in Kiswahili, which would seem to be a not inappropriate motto for the railway itself. Almost since the beginning, however, the train has been known as the Lunatic Express. Can't think why.

Man Eaters' Junction is so called, by the way, because in 1898 during the construction of the railway about 140 Indian workers were snatched and eaten by two lions (giving a whole new meaning to the term 'Indian take-away'). The railway's chief engineer, an ex-army man named Lt. Col. John H. Patterson, spent months trying to lure the lions into a trap (often using understandably reluctant Indians as bait), but always failed. On one notable occasion a junior employee named C. H. Ryall sat up all night in an open railway carriage with a rifle trained on a pile of bait outside, but unfortunately nodded off. The lions ignored the bait and took poor Ryall instead.

Finally, in early December, after nine months of frustration, Patterson managed to bag one of the lions. Three weeks later he shot and wounded the second one, which then bounded off into the bush. At first light the next morning he followed the trail of blood to the beast's lair. Though severely wounded, the lion charged. Patterson fired both barrels of his gun, and was nonplussed, to say the least, to find that the lion merely staggered sideways and then resumed coming for him. Turning to his rifle bearer for his backup gun, Patterson was additionally nonplussed to discover that the bearer was fifty feet away and climbing a tree. Patterson did likewise, just managing to haul himself onto a branch, the lion snapping at his quivering flanks. There he snatched the gun from the cowering bearer and fired once more, and the lion at last fell dead. The fate of the bearer is not recorded, but I believe we may reasonably assume that he was not further entrusted with the custody of firearms.

The journey from Nairobi to Mombasa takes thirteen hours, nearly all of it after dark, which is perhaps a mercy, all things considered. So long as it stays upright and settled on the rails, the train is quite wonderful. It was a little on the ancient side, to be sure, but we each had a snug private cabin, which looked comfortable enough, and the dining car was splendid, with a hearty three-course dinner and cheery, attentive service. Knowing the perils that lay ahead, we took the sensible precaution of anaesthetizing ourselves with many Tusker beers before, during and after dinner, but even so sleep was not to be found.

To begin with the beds were small and decidedly on the hard side, but it was the wild and extraordinary motions of the train that made even light dozing impossible. Normally I love overnight trips by train, but this was like trying to sleep through an earthquake. Even in its more tranquil spells, which were few, it was like being on one of those agitating conveyor belts that mining companies use to shake diamonds loose from piles of rubble. Because it was pitch dark outside, there was never any telling where we were, but the angle of the carriage made it evident that we were spending much of the night descending steeply. Every few hundred yards, or so it seemed, the driver would hit the brakes, setting off a chain reaction of collisions as each carriage slammed into the one ahead of it, followed a micro-instant later by the thuds and confused moans of people who have just been pitched out of bed. The experience would not have been a great deal different if they had put us all in a large barrel and rolled us to Mombasa.

TUESDAY, 1 OCTOBER

And so we stepped into the steamy morning heat of Mombasa, pleased to be back on solid ground. A vehicle from our hotel was waiting to whisk us up the coast to Malindi. Our principal task for the day was simply to get in position to fly on to Dadaab and a big CARE refugee camp the next day, but we had much to do in the meanwhile.

First we drove to a beach hotel north of Mombasa where

CARE people from all over Africa had gathered for a conference to thrash out a new five-year plan. There we dropped off David Sanderson, who was to address the conference before flying back to London, and picked up Nick Southern, CARE's regional manager for east Africa, whom I had met in London, as you will recall, and who was to be our host and protector for the next five days. An old Africa hand, Nick has been in Kenya for most of the past fifteen years and knows the country inside out.

With Nick collected, we resumed our journey up the coast, through a lush, tropical landscape of palm groves and endless sisal plantations (sisal is used to make rope, I was told) to a small resort called Watamu.

Watamu was tranquil to the point of being comatose. There were several good-sized hotels and associated businesses – diving shops and the like – but a decided paucity of holidaymakers. 'Tourism has really taken a beating here,' Nick said, 'especially the coastal resorts. If people want to see lions and giraffes, they still have to come to some place like Kenya, but if all they want is a beach holiday then they go to lots of other places.'

For a decade up to the mid-1990s, Kenya was a hot destination. International visitor numbers hit 850,000 in 1995, but then slumped to under 500,000 in 1997 amid a welter of bad publicity. Nearly everybody you meet can tell you some unnerving story about visitors coming to an unhappy end. Before I even came to Kenya I was told three different versions of a story about a German tourist who was either walking on a beach or sitting at an outdoor café or in a car at traffic lights with his arm out the window when someone lopped the arm off with a machete and ran off with the attached Rolex. The story is untrue, but that doesn't matter. What matters is that people believe it.

'When people hear these things and then someone says, "Oh and by the way you have to take malaria tablets, too," a lot of them decide just to go to Spain,' Nick said. 'It's a shame because Kenya's got so much going for it – beautiful countryside, lovely people, extraordinary wildlife, wonderful climate, great beaches. I mean, look,' he said and made a sweeping gesture across what was a setting of incomparable splendour: wide beach, nodding palms, bright sun, sparkling water.

We took a creaky glass-bottomed boat operated by two keen young men out to the reef about a quarter of a mile offshore and spent an hour admiring the large and colourful shoals of fish.

'Virtually the whole of the coast is reef like this,' Nick said. 'And they actually look after it pretty conscientiously.

ABOVE: Over 700,000 people live in Kibera, Nairobi, the largest slum in Africa.

RIGHT: Business as usual in Kibera.

LEFT: A girl in Kibera.

BELOW LEFT: Open drains and poor sanitation are an everyday problem.

BELOW RIGHT: A typical family home in Kibera.

ABOVE: Slum dwellers have little access to local services. Discarded rubbish is just one health hazard.

BELOW: Catching the train to Mombasa.

ABOVE LEFT: The craft market in the refugee camp, Dadaab.

ABOVE RIGHT: Making elaborate baskets for sale, Dadaab.

LEFT: A Somali girl in the refugee secondary school, Dadaab.

ABOVE: The fence is protecting valuable relief supplies.

BELOW: Relief food awaiting distribution to refugee families.

LEFT: Something to smile about –
a member of Wedco's loans group.

BELOW: A small extra loan made a big
difference to this family business.

ABOVE LEFT: A Wedco group busy selling fish from Lake Victoria in Kisumu market.

ABOVE RIGHT: The CARE-sponsored well brought clean drinking water to this village at Homa Bay.

RIGHT: With William Gumbo, a local champion of diverse farming.

The beautiful game:
Kisumu children and
their wonderful home-
made football.

For all they do wrong, the Kenyans manage wildlife very well.' He gave a slight apologetic shrug. 'You're seeing a lot of bad things this week. I thought it might be nice to see something good.'

'Thank you,' I said.

'And the next thing,' he went on, 'is really good. Have you ever heard of the Gedi ruins?'

'No,' I said without having to think.

'Not many people have. I think you'll be impressed.'

The Gedi ruins are inland from Watamu and down a winding track through enclosing overgrowth. From the thirteenth to seventeenth centuries Gedi was a thriving but oddly secretive community hidden away in a jungly setting in what was then a remote nowhere along the coast between Malindi and Mombasa. The inhabitants, who were Muslim, traded with people from all over the world. Archaeologists have found beads from Venice, coins from China, an iron lamp from India, and scissors from Spain, among a great deal else. But nowhere in any written records in any language does Gedi or its industrious people appear. Somehow for four hundred years Gedi interacted with the world without being noticed, and no one knows how it managed to escape attention or why it chose to.

Gedi wasn't rediscovered until the 1920s, by which time

it was completely overgrown, but excavations since then have uncovered mosques, tombs, houses, and a grand palace, spread across a forty-five-acre site. Monkeys run along the ruined walls, discreetly keeping an eye on visitors. The site still seems to half belong to the jungle, with mighty baobab trees growing up in what was once a busy lane or someone's sitting room. At the end of the day, with long sunbeams slanting through the forest, it was inexpressibly gorgeous. We were conducted around the site by Ali Abdala Alausy, the curator, a droll and cheerful man who was so clearly glad of visitors that he gave us what can only be called an exhaustive tour. There wasn't an alcove or pediment to which we weren't given a full history, not a pit or dwelling whose excavated contents weren't thoroughly described. We left packed with knowledge and admiration, and ready for a very large drink.

We spent the night at the Driftwood Beachclub Hotel, a stylish but conspicuously underutilized establishment standing on the Indian Ocean at Malindi. The only other customers in the large dining room were a family of four at a distant table – white Kenyans on holiday, Nick supposed.

Everybody was tired after the sleepless train journey of the night before, but even so we were unusually subdued.

I didn't realize it at the time but this was because, with the exception of Jenny, who fears nothing, we were all quietly certain we were going to die in the morning.

WEDNESDAY, 2 OCTOBER

A few years ago, I was on a scheduled flight on a sixteen-seater prop plane from Boston to my local airport in New Hampshire when the plane got lost in bad weather and couldn't find the airport. For forty minutes we flew around in a perplexed manner, occasionally dropping through the low clouds (which, I couldn't help noticing, we shared with many mountaintops) before the pilot got his bearings, or lucky, and put us on the runway with a descent so steep that I sometimes still sit upright in bed at 3 a.m. thinking about it. I vowed then that I would never go on another light aircraft. Then two years ago I flew in a light aircraft across Fiji almost, but not quite, ahead of the leading edge of the biggest tropical storm I ever hope to experience and I vowed then that really, absolutely and under no conditions would I set foot on a light aircraft again.

And now here I was about to fly 400 kilometres into bandit country in a charter plane in a Third World nation. I mentioned my reservations to Nick Southern at breakfast.

'I know just what you mean,' he said with feeling. 'I'm petrified myself.'

'That's not quite what I was hoping to hear,' I said.

'Absolutely bloody petrified,' he repeated for emphasis.

'I was rather counting on you to tell me everything is going to be fine, and that these planes never crash.'

'Oh, no, they crash all the time,' Nick said.

'I know they do, Nick. But I was hoping that you would tell me that somehow in Kenya they don't and that for some reason that hasn't occurred to me the world's most outstanding pilots come here to do charter work.'

Nick didn't seem to be listening to me any longer. 'Crash all the time,' he said. 'Poor Richard Leakey lost both his legs in a plane crash in Kenya, you know.'

'I'd heard that,' I said.

'And he was one of the lucky ones,' he added enigmatically.

Dan, also a piteous flier, arrived at the breakfast table just then. He was as white as a sheet, a condition somewhat exacerbated by the fact that he had inadvertently brushed his teeth with sun cream. Then poor Justin Linnane turned up looking similarly ghostly. He was uneasy because he had never been up in a small plane before and now learned that his début experience was to be in the company of the three most hysterical fliers in Africa. Only Jenny remained serene.

Thus it was that we were to be found an hour later at Malindi Airport, kicking the tyres of, and otherwise closely examining, the single-engine aircraft that was to convey us to CARE's refugee camp at distant, dusty Dadaab and thence, at the end of the day, to Nairobi.

The plane, I'm pleased to say, was quite new and looked sound, and the pilot, a man of great calmness named Nino, was undeniably sober and reliable looking. Under questioning he pointed out that he wanted to crash even less than we did since he would have to pay for the plane. I found this immensely reassuring. Best of all, it was a beautiful day for flying, the air still and almost cloudless. We were flying into the desert, after all, so the chances of storms were practically nil.

The flight itself proved blissfully uneventful. The engine purred steadily the whole way and no one took a shot at us. By the time we landed in Dadaab I was almost calm. Dadaab is bang on the Equator, in the middle of a dusty, orange nowhere, about sixty miles from the Somalia border. There has been a drought there for years, which is evident with every dry scrape of wind. In the early 1990s, refugees from the fighting in Somalia began to stream over the border into north-eastern Kenya, and a camp was hastily put together. Nearly a dozen years later it is home to 134,000 people.

The camp consists of three compounds, each a mile or two apart, and when travelling between any two you must be escorted by a truckload of Kenyan soldiers, just in case. The camp has become essentially a city in the desert, with schools and markets and permanent habitations. It has been there so long now that a generation of children has grown to adulthood without knowing any life other than being behind razor wire and heavy iron gates, and with a sense that all the world beyond this snug perimeter offers nothing but danger or indifference. CARE has 175 employees on site. Forty-five per cent of its spending in Kenya goes to the camp. Dadaab is a vivid reminder that refugee problems don't end simply because journalistic interest moves elsewhere. The inhabitants themselves are irremediably stuck. They can't go back to Somalia because it isn't safe and they can't go elsewhere in Kenya because Kenya has problems enough of its own without having 134,000 Somalis pitching up in Nairobi or Mombasa, looking for food and work. And so way out in the desert there exists this strange city-that-isn't-a-city filled with people who have nowhere to go and nothing much to do.

We spent a long day doing all the things you would expect to do at a refugee camp – toured the food distribution centre, visited schools, talked to administrators, learned how water was extracted from the ground and sanitized – but there was a curious lack of urgency about it all. The camp occupants weren't dying or malnourished or in desperate need of medical attention. They were just normal people like you and me who wanted to be somewhere where they could have a life.

Nearly everyone I spoke to complained of shortages of one kind or another – of work, of food, of teachers, of things to do. There are 28,000 pupils in the camp's schools, but only 807 desks. There is only one textbook for every twenty students, one classroom for every seventy-five. I talked to a bright young man named James Makuach, one of 357 students preparing to take the Kenyan Schools Certificate exam, a prerequisite for going on to higher education. He told me the school didn't have the facilities, in particular the scientific equipment, that would allow them to pass the test.

'You have no hope at all?' I said.

'Not much,' he said and gave me a heartbreakingly shy smile.

I couldn't understand this at all. I asked Nick – demanded really – why conditions weren't better than this. He looked at me with patient sympathy.

'There are twenty million like this all over Africa, Bill,' he said. 'Money only goes so far.' Besides, he went on, dispensing aid is much more complicated than most people realize. It is, for one thing, a fundamental part of aid protocol that you cannot make conditions notably better for refugees than they are for their hosts outside the camps. It wouldn't be fair and it would breed resentment. 'Everybody would want to be a refugee,' Nick said. 'In practical terms, you can only do so much.'

'But the kids,' I said. 'They have no future.'

'I know,' he said sadly. 'I know.'

Later, as we walked through the camp, Dan pointed out a nifty self-closing tap on a standpipe in the school grounds and told me that Nick had designed it, though he was too modest to say so. Nick, it turns out, is a water engineer by training and the tap was one of his first projects in Africa. You can find them all over Africa now, Dan told me.

Interestingly, nearly all the field workers for CARE were trained to do something else. David Sanderson was an architect before he became an aid worker. Adam Koons, whom we would meet in another day or so, was formerly a photographer on Madison Avenue in New York. A fellow now working in Ghana for CARE in a previous life designed the round teabag.

'People who work in the field are different from most of the rest of us,' Dan said as we strolled along. 'They live far away from their friends and families in places like this that are generally difficult and often dangerous, trying to help people they don't know to have better lives. Pretty remarkable really. Could you do that?'

'No,' I said.

'Neither could I.' He was thoughtful for a minute. 'But then I'd never have thought of the round teabag either.'

Late in the afternoon we returned to the airstrip for the ninety-minute flight to Nairobi. I asked Nino what the weather was like there.

'I'll let you know when we get closer,' he said vaguely, as if he weren't sharing all he knew.

Ten minutes before we arrived in Nairobi I found out why he was being coy. Ahead of us was a storm. It looked big. The thing about sitting near the front in a small aircraft is that you can see everything – to left, to right and straight ahead. None of it looked good.

We were over the outer suburbs of Nairobi and some way into our descent before we hit any turbulence – and it wasn't too bad. It didn't feel as if the wings were going to fall off or anything. But then the rain came – suddenly and noisily in staccato fashion. It was as if the windscreen were being pounded by wet bullets. Maybe it's always like that in the cockpit and you just don't know when you are in a separate compartment further back, but this was most assuredly unnerving. Worse, after a minute it became evident that Nino couldn't see a thing. He began to move his head from spot to spot around the windscreen, putting his nose to the glass, looking for any tiny bit of visibility. I couldn't understand why he didn't put the windscreen wiper on, then looked more closely and saw there wasn't a windscreen wiper. I glanced across at Nick and we shared a single telepathic thought: There's no windscreen wiper!

Actually two thoughts: There's no windscreen wiper and we're all going to die!

Nino was now bobbing around in his seat in the manner of someone who is trying to land an airplane while being attacked by fire ants. It appeared that from looking out the side window he could get a very rough fix on our location, but only very rough evidently because twice he banked sharply, as if swerving out of the path of a big building or something. This was rapidly becoming worse than my worst nightmare.

But still he pressed on. For one long minute, nothing much happened. We just flew forward in a seemingly straight line, continuously descending. When we were some small distance above the ground – seventy or eighty feet, say – and there was still nothing to be seen in front of us, I was pretty comfortably certain that we were going to die in the next few seconds. I remember being appalled, peeved even, but nothing more than that.

And then bang – and I use the word advisedly, of course – right before us, rushing at us at a ridiculously accelerated speed, was a runway. Nino tilted the plane and dropped us with the sort of suddenness that made our hats rise off our heads. We landed hard and decidedly off centre, and for a long moment – the one truly frightening moment of the whole episode – it seemed that he wouldn't be able to keep control, that we would hit the grass and somersault into a thousand pieces. But he managed to hold us steady and after a small eternity we came to a stop just outside a hangar.

'I'm naming my first child Nino,' Dan said quietly.

Nick was staring at his hand and a large piece of fuselage he seemed to have pulled off in the course of the landing.

Nino took off his headset and turned around beaming.

'Sorry about that, chaps,' he said. 'Had a little trouble spotting the runway.'

'W-w-why is there no windscreen wiper?' I asked with difficulty.

'They're no use with a single engine,' he said, pointing to the propeller directly in front. 'Best wiper in the world couldn't keep up with the spray off that thing.'

Somehow this didn't seem an entirely satisfactory explanation, but I was happy to leave it at that. Besides, I had a sudden overwhelming urge to drink my body weight in alcohol. And I can tell you this for certain now: however many years are left to me and wherever fate takes me, the only way I will ever be killed by a light aircraft is if one falls on me.

THURSDAY, 3 OCTOBER

And so to western Kenya. We set off bright and early to drive to Kisumu, Kenya's third city, on the shores of Lake Victoria. Kisumu is only about 300 kilometres west of Nairobi, but the roads are potholed and slow for much of the way, so we had to allow five hours to get there. I didn't care. None of us did. We were four feet off the ground and wouldn't get any higher all day.

The countryside was gorgeous – green and grassy with long views to the rugged Mau Escarpment in one direction and to the green hills of Aberdare National Park and central highlands in the other, all beneath vast blue skies and baking sun. Here and there along the heights overlooking the Rift Valley there were roomy laybys where you could pull off to take in the views, each with fifteen or twenty forlorn trinket and souvenir stalls waiting for customers who these days mostly never come. There was wildlife, too – families of baboons dining on road kill along the shoulder, herds of impalas and zebras dotting the grasslands, soda lakes carpeted with thousands of bright pink flamingos. There was no question that we were in Africa now. Kisumu has the distinction of being the poorest city in Kenya. Almost half the people live on fifty cents a day or less. Curiously, it looked more prosperous than many of the other places we had been. It had a trim, modern central business district and quite a lot of nice housing. There seemed to be more bicycles along the roads and fewer street urchins.

We had come to see the work of Wedco, a small bank – micro-finance institution is the formal term – that has been one of CARE's great success stories in the region. Wedco began in 1989 with the idea of making small loans to groups of ladies, generally market traders, who previously had almost no access to business credit. The idea was that half a dozen or so female traders would form a business club and take out a small loan, which they would apportion among themselves, to help them expand or improve their businesses. The idea of having a club was to spread the risk. It seemed a slightly loopy idea to many to focus exclusively on females, but it has been a runaway success.

'Our ladies are very shrewd and very hard working,' laughed Peres Oyugi, Kisumu's branch manager, as we drove to Kisumu's Jubilee Market to see some of Wedco's money in action. Ten years ago, she told me, Wedco had loans on its books of eighteen million Kenyan shillings – about $250,000. Today its loan portfolio has increased nearly tenfold to over 175 million shillings and it is helping more than 200 groups in Kisumu alone. There are seven other branches spread across the region.

Jubilee Market is an extraordinary place – crowded, noisy, extremely colourful – with large, open-sided halls specializing in wet fish, dried fish, vegetables, nuts and other farm commodities. I had never seen such luscious produce more beautifully arrayed. Every stall was a picture of abundance and sumptuousness, every peanut and tomato and chilli more neatly arranged and more richly coloured than any I had seen before anywhere. It seemed impossible that people so poor could enjoy such plenty. I asked Adam Koons, CARE's chief of operations for western Kenya, if it was as good as it looked.

'Oh, yeah,' he said. 'My wife and I do our own food shopping here. Kenyans haven't got much money, but they are very particular about their food.'

Beyond the main food halls was a sort of bazaar of dark alleys containing tiny shops – cubicles really – selling everything from bolts of cloth to small electrical items. There I was introduced to several of Wedco's happily prospering clients, among them a genial but weary-looking woman named Consolata Ododa. Ododa makes a living selling small oddments – batteries, torches, plastic wallets, key rings, playing cards. Like all the women in her group, Ododa works seven days a week, twelve hours a day, then goes home to cook an evening meal for her family, so it's not exactly a life of luxury. Every two weeks she makes an overnight trip to Nairobi by bus to acquire new stock, returning in time to reopen the stall late the following morning. She had just returned that day from her latest trip, and it was for this reason that she was 'a little tired', she told me. For all this her turnover averages about 3,000 shillings a day – roughly $30 – from which she must pay rent, electricity, taxes and interest and principal on her loan. Typically she will clear $6 or $7 for her twelve-hour day – hardly a princely sum, but more, she told me, than she had ever dreamed of having before Wedco stepped into her life. And so by such means do people's lives improve, little by little.

FRIDAY, 4 OCTOBER

Fifty miles or so south of Kisumu is Homa Bay, a listless small city of potholed streets, baking sun and an inescapable air of being at the wrong end of a long road. Most of the drive from Kisumu is along an exceedingly rough and bouncy dirt track. Interestingly, all road maps show it as a first-rate highway. This is because some years ago the World Bank gave money for the road to be paved. In the event, however, some government official or group of government officials decided to spare Kenyan workers the wearying toil of laying tarmac under a hot sun, and pocketed the money instead.

This sort of thing happens quite a lot in Kenya. Once a model of probity and rectitude, after twenty-three years under the government of Daniel arap Moi Kenya has become a case study in mismanagement and corruption. A group called Transparency International, which monitors global corruption, now ranks it as the sixth least trustworthy nation in the world, ahead of only Bangladesh, Nigeria, Paraguay, Madagascar and Angola. In one year, according to the BBC, ten billion dollars of public funds went missing in Kenya. Ten billion dollars! In one year! And it didn't even top the list!

Why institutions like the World Bank and IMF, not to mention our own slumbering governments, allow this to happen is a question I cannot answer, but it has unfortunate consequences for groups like CARE. First, it means that they are left to provide many of the services that any decent government would itself provide. It also means that donations for these services are harder to secure because so many people think that any money sent to Africa goes into the pockets of despots. If anyone ever, ever, ever tries to suggest to you that this is the case, you must poke them in the eyes with something at least as big as a snooker cue, for it just isn't so. Money given to aid agencies like CARE – and Oxfam and Save the Children and others beyond enumerating – doesn't pass through corrupt intermediaries. It goes straight into projects.

Incidentally, Moi is to step down in December when

elections are to be held. The universal hope, it appears, is that things will get better with a new government. 'They can't get worse,' I was told several times.

'It's not about spending huge amounts of money, but about spending smaller amounts intelligently,' Phillip Makutsa, one of CARE's project officers in the western province of Nyanza, told me as we bounced over more rough roads *en route* to the village of Ogongo Tir on the edge of the Lambwe Valley. He was explaining to me CARE's new philosophy with regard to aid, which was essentially twofold – to make a little go a long way and to help people to help themselves.

'It can be as little as narrowing the mouths of communal water containers so that people don't dip their hands into the water and accidentally contaminate it,' Phillip said. 'That one small step alone has produced a fifty-eight per cent decline in diarrhoeal outbreaks where implemented,' he added, beaming. We were arriving at Ogongo Tir. 'You'll see what I mean here,' he said.

Ogongo Tir was a scattered village in a green valley, which, thanks to CARE, boasted a new well. It was this that we had come to see. The well, it must be said, wasn't one of the wonders of the world. It was just a simple long-handled pump of the kind still commonly encountered at camp-grounds. My grandfather had one just like it, dating from about 1900, on his Iowa farm, so this was hardly cutting-edge technology. But what a difference it has made to Ogongo Tir's 321 households.

Before this, one of the village elders told me, during droughts and dry seasons women gathering water had to make a seven-hour round trip to a spring atop a steep and distant hill, setting out from the village at three in the morning in order to be back in time for the day's other chores. Because of the distance, none could carry more than a single five-gallon jerry can.

Now villagers have only to stroll to a clearing on the village edge to get safe, clean, adequate supplies of water. This was such a big deal to the community that the entire village turned out to greet us. Children sang us songs and their elders made speeches. Long speeches. Impassioned speeches. Speeches in Kiswahili and speeches in English. These were seriously grateful people.

'There's been a big change in how these things are done,' Nick told me as we were taken on a tour of a nearby vegetable garden, which blossoms even in the dry season thanks to water from the well. 'It used to be that we'd build a well for a village or make some other improvement and

then move on. Eventually, the pump would break or something would go wrong and the people wouldn't know
what to do. They'd come back to us and ask us to fix it
because they thought of it as our well.

'So the idea now is that we help them build the well,
but then the village takes complete responsibility for it.
They form a committee and run it as a kind of business.
They make a small charge for anyone who takes water so
that they then have a reserve fund for when they need to
make a repair or eventually dig a new well.'

'And has it worked?' I asked.

'Brilliantly, everywhere we've done it. It's amazing how
long it took aid agencies to figure out that people really,
really don't want dependency. They want to help themselves.'

'Only natural,' I observed wisely.

'Only natural,' he agreed.

We returned to our vehicles and plunged deeper into
the broad and comely Lambwe Valley. At length we stopped
at a small farm, where we met a sweet and eager young
farmer named William Gumbo. Gumbo owns four acres
of good but semi-arid land in the most gorgeous setting
in the very heart of the valley. It was almost uncannily
reminiscent of Tuscany or Provence – a place of dry, warm,

shimmering beauty. I can't tell you how much I wish you could have met William Gumbo, for he was an inspiration.

Until 1999 Gumbo scratched a living raising maize and millet and a few chickens. Then CARE stepped into his life. As part of its Dak Achana (Kiswahili for 'healthy households') programme, it introduced him to a couple of agricultural specialists, who showed him ways to increase his yields and diversify crops. Today he runs a model farm – a four-acre outburst of verdant plenty in the midst of a dry, bare valley. He grows peas, tomatoes, bananas, pineapples, passion fruit, mangos and much else. Only sweet potatoes have been a failure: some livestock broke through a fence and gobbled them up.

William Gumbo loves his farm. He carries a hardback ledger in which he records every detail of his plants' lives. Ask him about his banana trees and he will search through the book and tell you that he planted 310 of them on 20 April 2001, and then show you a weekly chronicle of their progress since. Everything is grown from seeds or cuttings. Nothing has been nursed on from a pot. It's all from scratch.

He showed us a grove of eucalyptus trees – 1,200 in all – that he has coaxed into being from seed. After a year and a half they are already fifteen feet tall. In another year and a half they will provide excellent wood for timber and poles. The same amount of land devoted to maize would produce about 16,000 Kenyan shillings in income over three years. The eucalyptus in the same period could produce as much as 200,000 shillings of income – over $2,500, a sum that most Kenyan farmers would find almost inconceivable.

The idea of the project is that CARE helps Gumbo create a model farm, then moves elsewhere. Gumbo, meanwhile, teaches what he has learned to his neighbours. Already he has helped 300 other farmers in the district.

The Lambwe Valley is not an easy place to prosper. It has long been notorious as one of the worst sites in east Africa for tsetse fly. The fly populations have been much reduced in recent years, but they still take a good number of animals. The valley is also cruelly drought prone. As of early October, it hadn't seen rain in over five months, so farming here will always be an uphill battle. Even if all goes well, William Gumbo will still be poor. His house has a dirt floor and it will be a very long time before he is luxuriating in shag-pile carpets. But he will probably have enough to buy his kids school uniforms – a prerequisite for attending even state schools in Kenya – or textbooks or pencils or a birthday present.

William Gumbo, in short, is a happy man and he has a future. Surely every human being is entitled to at least that much.

SATURDAY, 5 OCTOBER

Well, that's pretty much it, I'm afraid. We had another day in the countryside before we returned to Nairobi and flew home. We visited a tea plantation in Kericho, lunched with some jolly white farmers and toured a huge flower-growing operation on the shores of Lake Naivasha, but for me the trip ended with the happy villagers at Ogongo Tir and their beloved well, and with the heroic William Gumbo.

Obviously there is only so much you can learn about a country in eight days. We didn't have time even to visit many of CARE's projects in Kenya, and Kenya is only a small part of what it does. But I saw enough to realize that Kenya is a terrific country that is just full of William Gumbos and Consolata Ododas (the lady, you will recall, selling odd-ments at Kisumu's market) and Jillani Ngallas (the young man who longs to be a palaeontologist but probably will never make it) and thirty million other people just as individual and real. I don't suppose they can all be saintly and deserving, but they do have one thing in common with the rest of us: they are human beings. And, like us, they get only one life apiece, so naturally they tend to appreciate it – appreciate it very much, I believe – when people from a more comfortable part of the world take the trouble to help them make theirs better. For that's what CARE does, you see. It makes lives better, in sixty-four countries, thousands of times every day.

I don't know if you are fully aware of it, but in acquiring this slender volume you didn't actually buy a book. You made a generous donation to a worthy cause and got a free book in return, which isn't quite the same thing. It's much nobler. On behalf of CARE, thank you.

As I am sure the jacket conspicuously notes, my publishers, Transworld in Britain and Broadway in the United States, are also not taking a penny of profit from this – I know, I can hardly believe it myself – which means that a great many people behind the scenes worked hard for free to make this happen, and at the very busiest time of their working year. I think they deserve a special thanks, and most of your future purchases.

As for me and the rest of us in our party, well, we're very grateful too – grateful to the CARE people in Kenya for showing us around, and to you for your support. And best of all, not once in the week did we get rubbed with dung.

CARE INTERNATIONAL
SAYS THANK YOU

For buying *Bill Bryson's African Diary*. We hope you have enjoyed reading it.

This book has only been made possible because of the generosity and hard work of a range of people.

Thank you

To Dan McLean, Jenny Matthews, Justin Linnane, Kentice Tikolo, Nick Southern, Susan Onyango and David Sanderson who accompanied Bill on all or part of this journey and to everyone in CARE Kenya and CARE International UK, especially Chloe Bayram and Karen Kinross, who contributed their time, knowledge and skill to help make the journey a success.

Thank you

To all the people we met on our travels in Kenya, who

shared their experiences, who opened their hearts, minds
and, often, kitchens to us.

Thank you

To everyone at Transworld Publishers in London who
worked so hard to design, edit, typeset and promote this
book against a tight deadline, and who have so generously
donated all profits from sales to CARE International. Thank
you also to Broadway Books in New York who have also
donated all profits from US sales to CARE.

Thank you

To Cynthia Bryson and Carol Heaton for their patience and
support. And to Stanfords Travel Bookshop in London and
Richard Trillo at Rough Guides, for their support in pro-
moting and publicizing the book.

Above all, thank you

To Bill Bryson, the world's funniest, most generous and most
loved writer of people and places, who donated all royalties
from this book to CARE International and who withstood a
punishing schedule in a new country to produce his first
(but hopefully not last) African Diary.

CARE INTERNATIONAL WORLDWIDE

CARE International is an independent humanitarian agency working to end world poverty. CARE came into being at the end of the Second World War when American and Canadian citizens sent millions of 'CARE parcels' to feed hungry families in war-torn Europe and Asia. Today CARE International's programmes cover over sixty countries.

CARE's vision is a simple one: 'To overcome poverty and enable people to live in dignity and security.' Today, while many people live in affluence, extreme poverty affects more people than ever before, with 1.2 billion people existing on less than $US1 a day.

Each year CARE touches the lives of over thirty million people, helping them to escape poverty, improve their environment and participate in the decisions that affect their lives. But we don't work alone – our partners include local communities, governments, UN agencies and companies.

Every project funded by CARE International promotes sustainable solutions to the root causes of poverty and fosters community self-reliance to avoid long-term dependency. CARE programmes include water and sanitation, mother and child health, sustainable agriculture and small business development. Increasingly, we focus on projects that support poor communities in the overcrowded cities of the developing world.

CARE International also sends emergency food, shelter and supplies to survivors of natural disasters, wars and conflicts. We stay with communities long after initial relief efforts have ended, to help people rebuild their lives and face the future with confidence.

Why not support CARE's work? *See page 62 for details.*

MORE ABOUT CARE IN KENYA

CARE International began working in Kenya in 1968. For over thirty years, CARE has assisted communities in impoverished rural areas and city slums to gain access to essential services. CARE also provides life-saving relief in emergencies such as drought and floods, to refugees.

CARE's work in Kenya focuses on:

- CLEAN WATER AND GOOD SANITATION
- PRIMARY HEALTH CARE / HIV AIDS
- BASIC EDUCATION FOR DEPRIVED CHILDREN
- SUSTAINABLE AGRICULTURE FOR SMALL FARMERS
- ECONOMIC OPPORTUNITIES THROUGH MICROCREDIT AND BUSINESS TRAINING

Learn more on www.care.org

MOVING AHEAD WITH CARE

CARE International has always been a global movement and today we face our biggest challenge ever.

CARE's vision is to enable people to overcome poverty and live in dignity and security.

Our programmes aim to:

- ENABLE COMMUNITIES TO TAKE CONTROL OVER THEIR LIVES
- STRENGTHEN PEOPLE'S CAPACITIES FOR SELF-HELP
- CREATE ECONOMIC AND EDUCATIONAL OPPORTUNITIES
- GIVE PEOPLE THE TOOLS TO CHANGE THEIR LIVES FOR EVER.

We can only succeed with the support of people like you - people who care about the world they live in and want to end poverty. It will not be an easy process but it will be an absorbing and worthwhile one. We invite you to join us to end poverty.

To learn more about CARE and how to become involved

look at our global homepage: www.care.org and click on the CARE in your country.

Together we can build a better future.